Holy Baptism

The Lutheran Difference Series

Robert Rossow
with contributions by
Edward Engelbrecht

CONCORDIA PUBLISHING HOUSE · SAINT LOUIS

Copyright © 2003 Concordia Publishing House
3558 S. Jefferson Avenue
St. Louis, MO 63118-3968

All rights reserved. No part of this publication may be reproduced, stored in a retrieval system, or transmitted, in any form or by any means, electronic, mechanical, photocopying, recording, or otherwise, without the prior written permission of Concordia Publishing House.

Written by Robert Rossow with contributions by Edward Engelbrecht

Edited by Tom Doyle and Edward Engelbrecht

This publication may be available in braille, in large print, or on cassette tape for the visually impaired. Please allow 8 to 12 weeks for delivery. Write to the Library for the Blind, 7550 Watson Rd., St. Louis, MO 63119-4409; call toll-free 1-888-215-2455; or visit the Web site: www.blindmission.org.

All Scripture quotations are from the HOLY BIBLE, NEW INTERNATIONAL VERSION®. NIV®. Copyright © 1973, 1978, 1984 by International Bible Society. Used by permission of Zondervan Publishing House. All rights reserved.

Quotations from the *Concordia Triglotta* are © copyright 1921 by Concordia Publishing House. All rights reserved.

Manufactured in the U.S.A.

4 5 6 7 8 9 10 11 12 13   19 18 17 16 15 14 13 12 11 10

Contents

About This Series 5
Student Introduction 7
An Overview of Christian Denominations 11
Lutheran Facts 14

What Is Baptism? 15
What Baptism Bestows 21
What Baptism Does 27
Why Baptize Infants? 31
Living the New Life 37

Leader Guide Introduction 41
     Answers 43
Appendix of Lutheran Teaching 57
Glossary 60

About This Series

"I'm so excited! My brother asked me to be a godparent for my niece. She's getting baptized on Sunday."

"You mean the one who was just born? That isn't right. She's too young to be baptized."

"What do you mean?"

"She's too young to make a decision for Christ or even remember her Baptism. What good will it do her?"

As Lutherans interact with other Christians, they often find themselves struggling to explain their beliefs and practices. Although many Lutherans have learned the "what" of the doctrines of the church, they do not always have a full scriptural foundation to share the "why." When confronted with different doctrines, they cannot clearly state their faith, much less understand the differences.

Because of insecurities about explaining particular doctrines or practices, some Lutherans may avoid opportunities to share what they have learned from Christ and His Word. The Lutheran Difference Bible study series will identify how Lutherans differ from other Christians and show from the Bible why Lutherans differ. These studies will prepare Lutherans to share their faith and help non-Lutherans understand the Lutheran difference.

Student Introduction

- In the mid-1980s feminist theologians in the United Church of Canada raised questions about the words traditionally spoken at Baptism (Matthew 28:19). They proposed that, instead of using the masculine words "Father" and "Son," Baptisms should be done "in the name of the Creator and of the Redeemer and of the Sanctifier."
- Recently, Boulevard Baptist Church of Anderson, South Carolina, was dismissed from its local Southern Baptist Association. The Association dismissed the Boulevard congregation because it accepted as members Christians who had been baptized by pouring or sprinkling.
- When the Reformed Church of France, a mixture of Protestant groups, decided that it should offer the Lord's Supper to the "nonbaptized," Bishop Michel Viot resigned his office. He announced that he would convert to Roman Catholicism because the Reformed Church's decision undermined the Sacraments given by Christ.

Around the world the doctrine and practice of Baptism continues to complicate relationships between Christians. While some churches wish to de-emphasize Baptism in order to foster greater unity, other churches respond with revulsion to such proposals. They regard Baptism as so central to their identity that they reject such compromises for the sake of unity.

The reformer Dr. Martin Luther regarded Baptism as *the* identifying mark of a Christian. In fact, for Luther, Baptism *made* a Christian. Luther thought Baptism so central to the Christian faith that he encouraged fellow Christians to repeat the words of their Baptism each day.

As you begin this study of Baptism, recognize that you are studying one of the most controversial topics for Christians today. Prepare yourself for lively and intriguing discussion. But focus on what the Bible says and take special note of what the Bible does not say.

Much of the controversy about Baptism springs from a failure to focus on what the Lord actually says.

The Headwaters of Baptism

Jesus was not the first person to encourage Baptism. Nor was John the Baptist. The beginnings of Baptism spring from the Old Testament washings God commanded through Moses. To minister at the tabernacle, the priests needed to wash. Likewise, when the people visited the tabernacle for worship, they needed cleansing. Many ancient religions included ritual washing as part of their practice. But God made cleansing, purity, and holiness the focus of Old Testament life (Leviticus 11:44–45; 19:1–2; 20:7–8). You could not approach the Holy One of Israel if you were unclean.

After the Lord scattered the children of Israel among the nations because they broke His covenant, He promised that He would provide them with a new washing that surpassed the rituals of the old covenant. This washing would not simply purify the body. What's more important is that it would cleanse the heart, transform it, and bestow the Holy Spirit (Ezekiel 36:24–27).

As the people of Judah returned from exile in Babylon, they intermarried with the Gentiles who had settled in the land of Israel (Nehemiah 13:25–30). The rabbis were faced with the problem of purifying these foreigners. For boys and men, the old covenant provided a means of cleansing them and receiving them into the covenant: circumcision (Genesis 17). But the old covenant did not provide such a means for cleansing girls and women. It appears that the rabbis solved this problem by drawing on the Old Testament cleansing rituals. See *Infant Baptism in the First Four Centuries* by Joachim Jeremias (London: SCM Press LTD, 1960) pp. 24–40.

At any rate, ritual washing was part of conversion in Judaism in the first century before Christ, as demonstrated by the services of covenant renewal described in the Dead Sea Scrolls (The Community Rule, 1 QS III). For devout Jewish groups like the Essenes, ritual washing became a frequent or even daily religious practice (Mark 7:1–4, where "washing" is the Greek word for Baptism; note the plural in Hebrews 6:2). In fact, archaeologists have found ritual washing pools (Mikvehs) near the temple mount and at Qumran.

A New Covenant

When John the Baptist began calling the people of Judah to repentance, he was following the practice of devout people in his day. However, John's preaching showed that his baptism was different from the washings of other Jewish groups (Matthew 3:5–12). John's preaching and baptism were preparing the way for the coming of Jesus, for the new washing prophesied by Ezekiel and fulfilled in the New Testament (compare Ezekiel 36:24–27 with Jeremiah 31:31–33 and Hebrews 9:14–15). The Baptism provided by Jesus would make all other ritual washings obsolete.

As you dive into the New Testament's teaching about Baptism, bear in mind this Old Testament background and Ezekiel's prophecy. They will help you understand the full blessings of Baptism "in the name of the Father and of the Son and of the Holy Spirit" (Matthew 28:19).

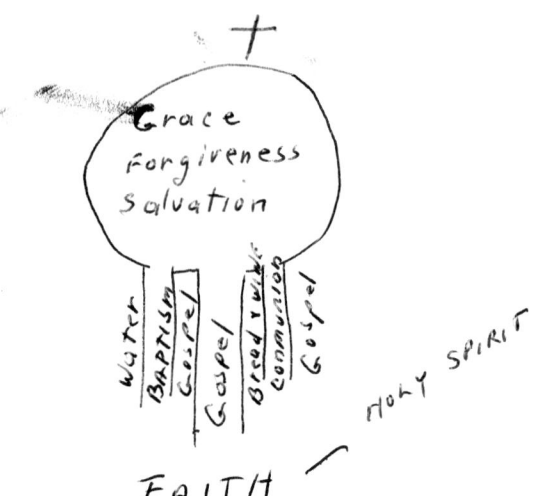

An Overview of Christian Denominations

The following outline of Christian history will help you understand where the different denominations come from and how they are related to one another. Use this outline in connection with the "Comparisons" sections found throughout the study. Statements of belief for the different churches are drawn from their official confessional writings.

The Great Schism

Eastern Orthodox: On July 16, 1054, Cardinal Humbert entered the Cathedral of the Holy Wisdom in Constantinople just before the worship service. He stepped to the altar and left a letter condemning Michael Cerularius, patriarch of Constantinople. Cerularius responded by condemning the letter and its authors. In that moment, Christian churches of the East and West were severed from each other. Their disagreements centered on what bread could be used in the Lord's Supper and the addition of the *Filioque* (Latin for "and the Son") statement to the Nicene Creed.

The Reformation

Lutheran: On June 15, 1520, Pope Leo X wrote a letter condemning Dr. Martin Luther for his Ninety-five Theses. Luther's theses had challenged the sale of indulgences, a fund-raising effort to pay for the building of St. Peter's Cathedral in Rome. The letter charged Luther with heresy and threatened to excommunicate him if he did not retract his writings within 60 days. Luther replied by publicly burning the letter. Leo excommunicated him on January 3, 1521, and condemned all who agreed with Luther or supported his cause.

Reformed: In 1522 the preaching of Ulrich Zwingli in Zurich, Switzerland, convinced people to break their traditional Lenten fast. Also, Zwingli preached that priests should be allowed to marry. When local friars challenged these departures from medieval church practice, the Zurich Council supported Zwingli and agreed that the Bible should guide Christian doctrine and practice. Churches of the Reformed tradition include Presbyterians and Episcopalians.

Anabaptist: In January 1525 Conrad Grebel, a follower of Ulrich Zwingli, rebaptized Georg Blaurock. Blaurock began rebaptizing others and founded the Swiss Brethren. Their insistence on adult believers' Baptism distinguished them from other churches of the Reformation. Anabaptists (*ana* means "again") attracted social extremists who advocated violence in the cause of Christ, complete pacifism, or communal living. Mennonite, Brethren, and Amish churches descend from this movement.

The Counter-Reformation

Roman Catholic: When people call the medieval church "Roman Catholic," they make a common historical mistake. Roman Catholicism as we know it emerged after the Reformation. As early as 1518 Luther and other reformers had appealed to the pope and requested a council to settle the issue of indulgences. Their requests were hindered or denied for a variety of theological and political reasons. Finally, on December 13, 1545, 34 leaders from the churches who opposed the Reformation gathered at the invitation of Pope Paul III. They began the Council of Trent (1545–63), which established the doctrines and practices of Roman Catholicism.

Post-Reformation Movements

Baptist: In 1608 or 1609 John Smyth, a former pastor of the Church of England, rebaptized himself by pouring water over his head. He formed a congregation of English Separatists in Holland, who opposed the rule of bishops and infant Baptism. This marked the start of the English Baptist churches, which remain divided doctrinally over the theology of John Calvin (Particular Baptists) and Jacob Arminius (General Baptists). In the 1800s the Restoration Movement of Alexander Campbell, a former Presbyterian minister, adopted many Baptist teachings. Churches coming from this movement include the Disciples of Christ (Christian Churches) and the Churches of Christ.

Wesleyan: In 1729 John and Charles Wesley gathered with three other men to study the Scripture, receive Communion, and discipline one another according to the "method" laid down in the Bible. Later, John Wesley's preaching caused religious revivals in England and America. Methodists, Wesleyans, Nazarenes, and Pentecostals form the Wesleyan family of churches.

Liberal: In 1799 Friedrich Schleiermacher published *Addresses on Religion* in an attempt to make Christianity appealing to people influenced by rationalism. He argued that religion is not a body of doctrines, provable truths, or a system of ethics, but that it belongs to the realm of feelings. His ideas did not lead to the formation of a new denomination, but they deeply influenced Christian thinking. Denominations or movements most thoroughly affected by liberalism are the United Church of Christ, the Disciples of Christ, and Unitarianism.

Lutheran Facts

All who worship the Holy Trinity and trust in Jesus Christ for the forgiveness of sins are regarded by Lutherans as fellow Christians, despite denominational differences.

Lutheran churches first described themselves as *evangelische*, or evangelical, churches. Opponents of these churches called them *Lutheran* after Dr. Martin Luther, the sixteenth-century German church reformer.

Lutherans are not disciples of Dr. Martin Luther, but rather are disciples of Jesus Christ. They proudly accept the name *Lutheran* because they agree with Dr. Luther's teaching from the Bible, as summarized in Luther's Small Catechism.

Lutherans may baptize by pouring, sprinkling, or immersing someone with water "in the name of the Father and of the Son and of the Holy Spirit." The mode of Baptism is usually decided by the setting and local custom, not by specific rules about how to apply the water.

When a person is baptized at a Lutheran church, that person is regarded as a member of the congregation and a member of the church universal.

Lutherans baptize people of all ages and all mental abilities, including infants and the mentally handicapped.

Though pastors usually administer Baptism, any layperson can baptize when special need arises (such as the imminence of death).

Following ancient church practice, Lutherans usually choose baptismal sponsors or "godparents" for the person being baptized. The role of a sponsor is to support and encourage the newly baptized person in the Christian faith (mentoring).

Today Lutherans usually baptize during the regular Sunday morning service.

When a person is baptized by another Christian church "in the name of the Father and of the Son and of the Holy Spirit," Lutherans regard this as a valid Baptism. They do not rebaptize.

To prepare for "What Is Baptism?" read John 1:1–34.

What Is Baptism?

They said our Christian gods were demons and that they would burn down our houses . . . [but] I am staying a Christian.

—Mr. Umra Mohan Pawar, Dangs, India, 1999

Many religions and cultures have special ritual washings. When a group of Hindu radicals poured water on Mr. Pawar and other Christians in India, they sought to undo their Christian Baptism. They gave Mr. Pawar a locket of the Hindu monkey god and told him that he was now a Hindu. But in the face of such bold persecution, Mr. Pawar quietly clung to his Baptism into Christ.

This Hindu ritual could not undo the blessings Mr. Pawar and other Christians receive in Baptism. God in His grace has chosen to come to us in simple means—water and the Word of Christ. His presence bears much power and bestows many blessings. A culture that seems obsessed with the extraordinary might not recognize God's extraordinary presence and promise in ordinary means—including Holy Baptism.

1. Describe a time God's profound presence and promise reached you through simple means.

2. Now describe a time God's profound presence and promise reached someone else through you.

God's Affinity for the Finite

A central teaching of the Bible is that the almighty, eternal God loved you and all people so much, He determined to reach you with His salvation.

3. Read John 1:14, 18. How far did God go to reach humanity?

become human   Gave up His only Son

4. What is the only way we can know God?

By faith through the Holy Spirit

5. Further affinities for finite manifestations of God's love are included in Scripture. Read each of the following passages and indicate by what ordinary means or manner God "showed up."

Exodus 3:1–6

Burning bush – angel

Mark 1:9–11

a dove

Matthew 21:1–11

King – a donkey

Matthew 13:34

Through parables

The Means of Grace

The "means of grace" are ways or vehicles through which God gives us His gifts—forgiveness of sins and eternal life. The means of

grace include God's ~~Word~~ Gospel and God's Sacraments of Holy Baptism and the Lord's Supper. Scripture teaches that the Sacraments
- are instituted and commanded by God (Matthew 28:19);
- include a visible element connected with God's Word (Ephesians 5:26);
- convey God's grace, the promise of forgiveness of sins, and eternal life through faith in Christ Jesus (Galatians 3:26; Acts 2:38–39).

6. What makes God's means of grace such incredible gifts?

It is free. Gives us eternal life

Holy Baptism

7. Read Matthew 28:19–20. Who commanded Baptism?

Jesus

8. Who is to be baptized?

Everyone. All nations

9. Read Titus 3:5–6. What is God's attitude toward us?

He loves us and shows us His mercy

10. What is the basis of our salvation?

Baptism (Washing of rebirth and renewal by the Holy Spirit) God's Grace in Christ who died and rose again

11. What does "washing of rebirth" (v. 5) refer to?

Baptism

Lost and Found

When the children of Israel left their homeland and settled in Egypt (c. 1875 B.C.), they forgot about God's promises to their forefathers. They were lost until the Lord spoke to Moses and called him to preach to the people and lead them out of Egypt. Instead of appearing to the leaders of Israel, God chose to reach Israel through an 80-year-old sheepherder, Moses.

12. God has told us that He communicates His presence and power through rather simple means. Where should we be looking for God? How has God found you? *In everything we see & do. Everywhere His word & sacraments*

13. Describe what God has provided for you and continues to provide for you through simple means. *Food, clothing, shelter, forgiveness, life in salvation; strengthing the faith in God's grace*

14. How would you respond to someone who claimed that Baptism is only a church tradition with simple symbolic qualities? *It is when the Holy Spirit comes into my life. Jesus Commanded baptism*

Live in Your Baptism

To do this week:
- Gratefully acknowledge in prayer the gifts you received at your Baptism. If you are not baptized, pray about receiving Baptism.
- Become more aware of biblical accounts of God "showing up" in ordinary ways.
- Talk with your children (or someone close) about the significance of Baptism.

Comparisons

Most Christian churches regard Baptism as a sacrament. They teach that God bestows grace through Baptism. Eastern Orthodox, Lutheran, Roman Catholic, Episcopal, Reformed, and some Wesleyan churches hold to a sacramental view.

Eastern Orthodox: "What virtue is there in each of these Sacraments? In Baptism man is mysteriously born to a spiritual life" (Longer Catechism of the Eastern Orthodox Church, question 286).

Lutheran: "The Sacrament of Holy Baptism . . . [is] a life-giving water, rich in grace, and a washing of the new birth in the Holy Spirit" (Luther's Small Catechism with Explanation, pp. 21–22).

Roman Catholic: "If any one saith that in the Roman church, which is the mother and mistress of all churches, there is not the true doctrine concerning the sacrament of baptism; let him be anathema" (Council of Trent, Seventh Session, On Baptism, Canon 3).

Reformed: "Baptism is a sacrament of the New Testament, ordained by Jesus Christ, not only for the solemn admission of the party baptized into the visible Church; but also, to be unto him a sign and seal of the covenant of grace" (The Westminster Confession of Faith, chapter XXVIII.1).

Methodist: "Sacraments ordained of Christ are...certain signs of grace, and God's good will toward us, by which he doth work invisibly in us, and doth not only quicken, but also strengthen and confirm, our faith in him. There are two Sacraments ordained of Christ our Lord in the Gospel; that is to say, Baptism and the Supper of our Lord" (Methodist Articles of Religion, article 16).

Some Christian churches hold that Baptism is an ordinance. They view Baptism as a public declaration of faith and commitment, which only the mature should receive. Anabaptists, Baptists, and some Wesleyans hold to an ordinance view.

Baptist: Baptism is an ordinance of the New Testament, ordained by Jesus Christ, to be unto the party baptized as a sign of his fellowship with him, in his death and resurrection (1689 London Baptist Confession of Faith, Chapter 29: Of Baptism, 1).

Anabaptist: "[Leaders of the church should] be an example, light, and pattern in all godliness and good works, worthily administering the Lord's ordinances—baptism and supper" (Dordrecht Confession, article IX).

Point to Remember

He saved us through the washing of rebirth and renewal by the Holy Spirit, whom He poured out on us generously through Jesus Christ our Savior, so that, having been justified by His grace, we might become heirs having the hope of eternal life. Titus 3:5b–7

To prepare for "What Baptism Bestows," read Romans 6:3–11.

What Baptism Bestows

Even as a boy I had heard of eternal life promised to us through the humility of the Lord our God condescending to our pride . . . I solicited from the piety of my mother, and of Thy Church, the mother of us all, the baptism of Thy Christ, my Lord and my God.
—St. Augustine, *Confessions,* chpt. XI:17

To appreciate the special quality of Baptism, you must first understand the depth of human need. Paul wrote, "For the wages of sin is death, but the gift of God is eternal life in Christ Jesus our Lord" (Romans 6:23). When it comes to our relationship with God all we "bring to the table" is sin and death. But God brings the gift of eternal life in Christ.

15. When have your thoughts, words, or deeds made you feel guilty?

16. What assurance did you find in God's unconditional love for you?

The Greatest Gifts

17. Read Acts 2:38–39. What two gifts are mentioned in connection with Baptism?

18. To whom does God give these gifts?

19. Read Romans 5:8. How did the gift of salvation start?

20. Read 1 Corinthians 1:30. From where does our righteousness before God come?

21. Read 2 Corinthians 5:21. What had to happen in order for us to be declared righteous?

22. Read Ephesians 2:8 and Titus 3:3–7. How do we receive Christ's righteousness?

23. Read Romans 6:3–11. What died with Christ in our Baptism?

24. What rose with Christ in our Baptism?

25. Read Colossians 1:13–14. What does the "dominion of darkness" refer to?

26. How has God rescued us from it?

Comfort in Christ

27. As demonstrated above, Scripture clearly connects the forgiveness of sins with Baptism. How would you respond to someone who claimed that Baptism is only a symbol or confession of faith by the person baptized?

28. What active role does a person play in receiving the forgiveness of sins?

29. We were buried with Christ through Baptism into death. And just as Christ was raised, so we, too, are raised to a new life (Romans 6:3–4). What comfort does this biblical truth bring to you when your sins weigh heavily upon you?

Rejoice in Your Baptism

To do this week:
- Read "The Sacrament of Holy Baptism" in Luther's Small Catechism.
- Confess that all your sins were buried in Christ's death.
- Record the date of your Baptism and the Baptisms of other family members on the family calendar. Plan Baptism celebrations, just as you would plan birthday celebrations.

Comparisons

Eastern Orthodox, Lutheran, Roman Catholic, and some other churches teach that God bestows salvation or new birth through Baptism. (*Regeneration* is from a Latin term meaning "born again.")

Eastern Orthodox: "Baptism is a Sacrament, in which a man…is born again of the Holy Ghost to a life spiritual and holy" (The Longer Catechism of the Eastern Orthodox Church, question 288).

Lutheran: "Baptism . . . [is] a life-giving water, rich in grace, and a washing of the new birth in the Holy Spirit" (Luther's Small Catechism with Explanation, p. 22).

Roman Catholic: Through Baptism we are born again and made members of the church. It is the gateway to the whole Christian life.

Reformed churches teach that Baptism places a person in a covenant relationship with God.

Reformed: "Baptism . . . doth signify and seal our ingrafting into Christ, and partaking of the benefits of the covenant of grace, and our engagement to be the Lord's" (Westminster Shorter Catechism, question 94).

Anabaptist, Baptists, and some Wesleyans regard Baptism as a symbol of a person's personal commitment to Christ and a new way of life.

Baptism: "We believe that Christian Baptism is the immersion in water of a believer, into the name of the Father, and Son, and Holy Ghost; to show forth in a solemn and beautiful emblem, our faith in the crucified, buried, and risen Savior" (New Hampshire

[Baptist] Confession of Faith, declaration 14).

Anabaptist: "Concerning baptism we confess that penitent believers who, through faith, regeneration, and the renewing of the Holy Ghost, are made one with God, and are written in heaven, must, upon such Scriptural confession of faith, and renewing of life, be baptized with water" (Dordrecht Confession, article VII).

Point to Remember

We were therefore buried with Him through Baptism into death in order that, just as Christ was raised from the dead through the glory of the Father, we too may live a new life. Romans 6:4

To prepare for "What Baptism Does," read Galatians 3:22–4:7.

What Baptism Does

We are CHRISTians.

—Missionary Harley L. Kopitske

Mankind's identity is by nature connected with the Old Adam and is defined by sin and death. To be redefined by righteousness and life, we need a new identity—one that is connected with the New Adam, Christ Jesus. Baptism provides this new connection and new life.

Since medieval times, Christians have used another name for Baptism: Christening. This special term reminds Christians of what Baptism does. It gives them a new identity, uniting them with Christ.

30. There's an old saying that goes, "Show me your friends and I'll show you your future." Think of a time in your life when the company you kept tarnished or polished your identity.

31. Describe a time when you experienced the profound realization that you are a child of God. How did this change the way you felt and acted?

The Garment of Salvation

32. Read Titus 3:5–8. Who saved us?

33. Why are we saved?

34. What means did God use to convey His saving grace?

In every culture clothing and jewelry provide important means for identifying who people are and what they do.
35. Read the following items and list or discuss what identity they convey:

    a suit   a crown

    a cross   sneakers

    coveralls   black robes

36. Read Galatians 3:26–27. What does it mean to be clothed with Christ?

37. What no longer defines our identity? What does define our identity (see Galatians 5:24)?

38. Based on your outward actions, how might people identify your faith? Why?

39. Read Ephesians 4:22–23. What are some of the characteristics of the "old self"?

40. Based on Galatians 5:22–26, what attitudes and actions might flow from our identity in Christ Jesus?

The New You

41. Many people search for identity or go on a quest to "find themselves." Where would you direct a fellow Christian who is struggling with such a search?

42. In today's fashion-obsessed world "you are what you wear." How could this misguided perception actually help us understand our true spiritual identity?

43. What symbol often used at the Baptism of a child draws attention to "putting on" Christ?

Flaunt Your Faith

To do this week:
- Thank God in prayer for making you alive in Baptism.
- Remind yourself that you have "put on" Christ by making the sign of the cross "in the name of the Father and of the Son and of the Holy Spirit" (see Luther's Small Catechism, Daily Prayers).
- Strive to live and act in a way that other people can see your real identity—in Christ Jesus.

Comparisons

Revivalism: In some Protestant church bodies, people are baptized numerous times, each time they experience a religious conversion and wish to declare the new direction for their lives.

One Baptism: Most churches teach that Baptism makes a person a member of the kingdom of God—His church—despite denominational affiliation. These churches do not rebaptize people who have been properly baptized by a different church (e.g., a Lutheran would not rebaptize a person baptized in the Roman Catholic church).

Anabaptism: During the sixteenth century, churches that believed in adult Baptisms only insisted that people baptized as infants be rebaptized as a testimony to their faith. Anabaptists, Baptists, and some Wesleyans practice rebaptism.

Point to Remember

For all of you who were baptized into Christ have clothed yourselves with Christ. Galatians 3:27

To prepare for "Why Baptize Infants?" read Colossians 2:9–15.

Why Baptize Infants?

Today you will be baptized a Christian. All those great ancient words of the Christian proclamation will be spoken over you, and the command of Jesus Christ to baptize will be carried out on you, without your knowing anything about it.

—Dietrich Bonhöffer, *Letters and Papers from Prison*

From a Nazi prison in 1944, Pastor Bonhöffer wrote his newborn nephew, Dietrich Wilhelm, a letter for the day of his Baptism. It would be years before Dietrich Wilhelm could understand or read this letter for himself. For cynical minds, Pastor Bonhöffer's letter may seem like a waste of effort, a waste of words.

But words are not so powerless. Pastor Bonhöffer realized that he was passing on to his nephew a heritage and inheritance through the counsel and encouragement of words. With this letter, he left something of enduring value for his nephew.

44. A newborn baby cannot understand the words of its parents' lullaby or the legal implications of its parents' will. Does that mean parents should not sing lullabies or prepare wills with their children as beneficiaries? Why or why not?

Those who object to the practice of infant Baptism often do so because they believe infants
- don't need it (condition of innocence);
- can't understand what they are doing or receiving (condition of noncognition);
- are incapable of deciding or willing Baptism (condition of nonvolition). *not yet capable of faith*

Those who object to infant Baptism fail to recognize the dire need of all people because of sin. They likewise fail to appreciate the power of God's Word. Scripture clearly states that all people, including

Not accountable
cannot believe
1) Won't have a meaning later in life.
2) When was Jesus baptized.

31

Luke 18:15

infants, are diseased with the condition of sin (Romans 3:10–18, 23). Because of sin the human reason and the will are *always* hostile to God. They do not preclude God's ability to convey His grace.

45. Who decided that you were to be born?

Parents

46. Consider the character of adoption. What rights and privileges does a child receive in adoption?

The name & all the rights & privileges of a birth child

47. What part does an infant play in determining who adopts and what rights and privileges he or she receives through adoption?

Dead in Sin

48. Read Psalm 51:5 and Romans 5:18–19. According to the psalmist, when does the condition of sin begin?

49. From whom did we inherit our condition of sin?

Adam & Eve & our parents

50. Whose obedience is responsible for our righteousness?

Christ

51. Read Matthew 19:14. What is Jesus' attitude toward children?
He loves them

52. Read John 3:3–5; *John 3:3* Luke 12:32; and Ephesians 2:8. How do people receive the kingdom of heaven?
Rebirth through baptism

53. If the kingdom of heaven belongs to little children, and the kingdom of heaven is received by faith, then what may we conclude about the capacity of little children to have faith? *Matthew 18:6...*

54. Read John 1:12–13. If parents make the decision for a child's natural birth, who makes the decision for a child's spiritual birth?

55. What can Christian parents do for their infants to facilitate God's gracious decision?

Our Inheritance

56. Children inherit physiological and psychological traits from their parents. Consider yourself and your family in particular. What spiritual trait did you inherit from your parents?

Infant Baptism: God does the work (what God does)
adult " : We do the work (what we do)

Scripture reveals who should and should not receive the Sacrament of the Lord's Supper (1 Corinthians 11:28–32). We do not find similar specifications concerning Baptism.

57. Do you think such silence supports the practice of infant Baptism? Why or why not?

Faith cannot be reduced to a cognitive understanding or an articulate confession of the Christian faith, although ordinarily it includes both. Faith, in its simplest form, is trust that clings to God's promises. The Holy Spirit, working through Baptism, elicits such a trust in infants.

58. What would you say to a friend or relative who is planning to wait to have her or his child baptized until the child is old enough to decide?

The Family of Faith

To do this week:
- Gratefully acknowledge that you have been adopted into God's family by grace.
- Read the Order of Holy Baptism found in *Lutheran Worship* (pp. 199–204).
- Pray for your children and the children of others that they might grow in their faith and appreciate the blessings they have received in their Baptism.

Comparisons

Eastern Orthodox, Lutheran, Roman Catholic, Reformed, and some Wesleyan churches baptize infants as well as adults (including the mentally handicapped). These churches note that Jesus does not put an age limit on Baptism (Matthew 28:19). They view the Bible references to "household" Baptisms as including people of all ages (Acts 11:14; 16:15, 33; 18:8; the Greek term for "household" included every resident of a house, including servants and their families).

Eastern Orthodox: "How can you show from holy Scripture that we ought to baptize infants? In the time of the Old Testament, infants were circumcised when eight days old; but Baptism in the New Testament takes the place of circumcision; consequently infants should be baptized" (The Longer Catechism of the Eastern Church, question 293).

Lutheran: "That the Baptism of infants is pleasing to Christ is sufficiently proved from His own work, namely, that God sanctifies many of them who have been baptized, and has given them the Holy Ghost" (Large Catechism, Baptism, paragraph 49).

Roman Catholic: "If any one saith that little children, for that they have not actual faith, are not, after having received baptism, to be reckoned amongst the faithful; and that, for this cause, they are to be rebaptized when they have attained to years of discretion . . . , let him be anathema" (Council of Trent, Seventh Session, On Baptism, Canon 13).

Reformed: "Are infants also to be baptized? Yes: for since they, as well as the adult, are included in the covenant and church of God; and since redemption from sin by the blood of Christ, and the Holy Ghost, the author of faith, is promised to them no less than to the adult; they must therefore by baptism, as a sign of the covenant, be also admitted into the Christian Church" (The Heidelberg Catechism, question 74).

Methodists: "The baptism of young children is to be retained in the church" (Methodist Articles of Religion, article 17).

Anabaptists, Baptists, and some Wesleyans baptize only those who are mature enough to state their faith and express a desire for Baptism (teen years or late childhood at the earliest). They point out that particular examples of Baptism describe adult participants and do not explicitly mention children.

Some teach a particular "age of accountability." They teach that before this age, God does not hold people accountable for things they do wrong.

Baptist: "Those who do actually profess repentance towards God, faith in, and obedience to, our Lord Jesus Christ, are the only proper subjects of this ordinance" (1689 London Baptist Confession of Faith, Chapter 29: On Baptism, 2).

Anabaptist: "Concerning baptism we confess that penitent believers, who, through faith, regeneration, and the renewing of the Holy Ghost, are made one with God, and are written in heaven, must, upon such Scriptural confessions of faith, and renewing of life, be baptized with water" (Dordrecht Confession, article VII).

Point to Remember

Peter replied, "Repent and be baptized, every one of you, in the name of Jesus Christ for the forgiveness of your sins. And you will receive the gift of the Holy Spirit. The promise is for you and your children and for all who are far off—for all whom the Lord our God will call." Acts 2:38–39

To prepare for "Living the New Life," read Colossians 2:3–12; 3:1–17.

Living the New Life

—I am baptized.

Dr. Martin Luther, Large Catechism, Baptism, para. 44

Martin Luther would tell people, "I *am* baptized" (present passive verb) rather than "I *was* baptized." By this he meant that Baptism affects our ongoing identity. It is not simply an isolated and ineffectual act of the past. Baptism defines both who we are and what we do now.

59. What does it mean to "remember your roots"?

60. What kinds of attitudes and behaviors are associated with the Christian life?

New Creation

At the dawn of creation the Lord said, "Let there be light" (Genesis 1:3). Since that moment light has shone forth, making life possible and perpetually sustaining life.

61. Read 2 Corinthians 3:18 and 4:6. Who shines the light? What are the results?

62. How is this light often symbolized at a Baptism?

A Change for the Better

63. Read Ezekiel 36:24–27 and Titus 3:4–7. How does Baptism change our hearts?

64. Read Colossians 2:12–13a; 3:1–2. How does Baptism change our minds?

65. Read Colossians 3:5–17. How does Baptism change our behavior?

66. Read Acts 2:38–39. What promises received in our Baptism can we remember?

67. Read Hebrews 10:22–25. What can we do to facilitate such remembering?

One in Christ

68. Read 1 Corinthians 6:11. The Holy Spirit washed and sanctified us at our Baptism. Whose guidance should we seek to help us live the new life?

A change of identity translates into a change in living. This does not always mean that we do new things. Sometimes it simply means that we do the same things better.

69. In what specific areas of your life would you like to see a change for the better?

70. Regular church attendance facilitates remembering your Baptism. What particular parts of the Divine Service help you personally to remember your Baptism?

Created for Life

To do this week:
- Thank the Holy Spirit for creating a new life in you.
- Pray that the Holy Spirit would enable you to have a more loving heart, a more Christ-centered mind, and a more godly lifestyle.
- Remember your Baptism as you worship.

Comparisons

Confirmation. Churches that baptize infants also practice confirmation (Eastern Orthodox, Lutheran, Roman Catholic, Reformed, and some Wesleyan churches). Based on Matthew 10:32–33; 28:19–20, Lutheran children are expected to receive diligent instruction in the teachings of the Christian faith, leading to a public confession of Jesus Christ.

Point to Remember

Let us draw near to God with a sincere heart in full assurance of faith, having our hearts sprinkled to cleanse us from a guilty conscience and having our bodies washed with pure water. Hebrews 10:22

Leader Guide

Leaders, please note the different abilities of your class members. Some will easily find the Bible passages listed in this study. Others will struggle. To make participation easier, team up members of the class. For example, if a question asks the class to look up several passages, assign one passage to one group, the second to another, and so on. Divide up the work! Let participants present the different answers they discover.

Each topic is divided into four easy-to-use sections.

Focus introduces key concepts that will be discovered.

Inform guides the participants into the Scriptures to uncover truths concerning a doctrine.

Connect enables participants to apply what is learned in Scripture to their lives and provides them an opportunity to formulate and articulate a defense of a key doctrine.

Vision provides participants with practical suggestions for extending the theme of the lesson out of the classroom and into the world.

Also take note of the Comparisons section at the end of each lesson. The editor has drawn this material from the official confessional documents and historical works of the various denominations. The passages describe and compare the denominations so that students can see how Lutherans differ from other Christians and how all Christians share many of the same beliefs and practices. The passages are not polemical.

What Is Baptism?

Objectives

By the power of the Holy Spirit working through God's Word, participants will (1) describe how God on many occasions appeared to His people through simple means, (2) affirm that God has promised His church to communicate His presence and promise through the simple means of Word and Sacrament, and (3) confess how through Baptism God comes to His children with the promise of forgiveness and eternal life.

Opening Worship

Sing or speak together stanza 4 of "To Jordan Came the Christ, Our Lord" (*LW* 223).

Focus

Read aloud the introduction. Ask for responses to the two questions.

1–2. Answers will vary. Draw attention to our Lord's promise to come to us in His Word and Sacraments. Also remind participants that God can reach others through them and their everyday encounters in how they live and speak.

God's Affinity for the Finite (Inform)

3. God became human in Christ (incarnation) to reach us and to remedy our sinful condition.

4. Although we can learn things about God through the beauty, power, and order of creation, we can only know God through Christ.

5. Exodus 3:1–6—God appears in a burning bush. Mark 1:9–11—God the Holy Spirit appears like a dove and the Father's voice is heard. Matthew 21:1–11—God the Son appears riding on a donkey. Matthew 13:34—God the Son communicates the kingdom of God through words (parables).

The Means of Grace

6. Through the means of grace God creates saving faith in Christ Jesus and strengthens and preserves the faith of believers.

Baptism means a washing with water (Matthew 28:19–20). Discuss the spiritual implications of this meaning in light of Baptism—the washing of our sins.

Holy Baptism

7. God Himself commanded Baptism.

8. All nations are included in the command to baptize. This means all kinds of people without respect to nationality, age, or ability; "All nations" means God gave Baptism as a blessing for everyone.

9. God's attitude is one of kindness and love.

10. Our salvation is not based on our worth or merit but only in God's mercy for the sake of Christ.

11. The "washing of rebirth" refers to the Sacrament of Holy Baptism.

Lost and Found (Connect)

12. We are to look for God where He promised to be—in His Word and Sacraments. Regular devotion time and worship provide us with the opportunity to encounter God and His promises, as do the receiving of the Lord's Supper and the remembering of Baptism.

13. God found us and claimed us through the Gospel—the visible Gospel in Holy Baptism or from the spoken Gospel heard and then received in faith. Through simple means God provides the creation of saving faith in Christ Jesus and the strengthening of that faith, which clings to the gifts of forgiveness of sins and eternal life.

14. God instituted and commanded Holy Baptism; through it He provides forgiveness of sins and eternal life.

Live in Your Baptism (Vision)

Encourage participants to complete one or more of the suggested activities.

What Baptism Bestows

Objectives

By the power of the Holy Spirit working through God's Word, participants will (1) confess that through Christ, God provided the forgiveness of sins (objective justification) for all people, (2) describe how people receive this forgiveness by faith (subjective justification), and (3) confess that Baptism is one of the means through which people subjectively receive this objective gift.

Opening Worship

Sing or speak together the first stanza of "I Am Trusting You, Lord Jesus" (*LW* 408).

Focus

Read aloud the introduction. Ask for responses to the two questions.

15–16. Answers will vary. Draw attention to people's habit of rationalizing their sinful condition as well as their sinful actions. When all such rationalizations are stripped away, people find assurance of God's love and mercy in His Word. Remind the students that God's love and mercy is communicated to us in Baptism. Thus, remembering our Baptism edifies and assures us.

The Greatest Gifts (Inform)

17. Forgiveness of sins and the gift of the Holy Spirit are received in Holy Baptism. The punctuation in some translations of these verses can be misleading. Verses 38–39 are one sentence in Greek,

emphasizing that both forgiveness *and* the Holy Spirit are bestowed in Baptism "for you and your children."

18. Note the apostle's words. The promise of these gifts is for all—young and old. Age is not the important factor. The calling of God in Christ is what Peter emphasizes.

19. God's gift of forgiveness flows from His love for us in Christ rather than from our love for Him.

20. Our righteousness comes to us from outside of ourselves—only through Christ Jesus.

21. God declares us righteous only for the sake of Christ. Jesus was declared guilty in our place.

22. God accomplished and conveyed our salvation (forgiveness and eternal life) entirely by His grace. Nothing we are or do merits His gifts. We receive forgiveness of sins and eternal life through faith in the merits of Christ Jesus won for us on the cross.

23. Our old self and its slavery to sin died with Christ in our Baptism.

24. A new life rose with Christ in our Baptism. This new life occurs even now as we receive Christ's righteousness and will be finally and fully received on Judgment Day.

25. The "dominion of darkness" refers to the power of the devil and all of his evil.

26. By Christ's death on the cross, God prepared our rescue from the devil's kingdom. Baptism delivers us from the power of the devil and shields us from all the evil accusations of the old evil foe. Christ took these accusations with Him to the cross.

Comfort in Christ (Connect)

27. Through Holy Baptism God comes with His love in Christ through His Word. Any confession of faith accompanying this act of God is purely a response to God's grace.

28. A person plays no active role in receiving the forgiveness of sins. God acts to redeem us through Jesus Christ. God declares His mercy upon us for the sake of Christ. In other words, God creates and sustains our faith.

29. Our sin was buried with Christ. Now we need to let those old, dead, buried sins rot, and not bring them back to life. Christ and His

righteousness are alive in us. Setting our hearts and minds on Christ brings much comfort.

Rejoice in Your Baptism (Vision)

Encourage participants to complete one or more of the suggested activities.

What Baptism Does

Objectives

By the power of the Holy Spirit working through God's Word, participants will (1) confess that God makes people alive through Baptism, (2) describe how through Baptism people "put on" Christ, and (3) live in their Baptism as they "put off" their old selves.

Opening Worship

Sing or speak together stanzas 3 and 4 of "All Mankind Fell in Adam's Fall" (*LW* 363).

Focus

30–31. Answers to the questions will vary. Emphasize that in Baptism, *God* acts, not us. We passively receive His active grace. Also redirect participants' attention from any merits and worthiness in themselves to the merits and worthiness Christ earned for them on the cross.

The Garment of Salvation (Inform)

32. God saved us in Christ.

33. Our salvation is based not upon who we are or what we do. Rather, God's love moved Him to save us for the sake of His Son, Jesus Christ.

34. God saved us "through the washing of rebirth and renewal by the Holy Spirit"—Holy Baptism. This washing produces in us a faith that clings to the merits of Christ.

35. Answers may vary. A list may state that a businessperson wears a suit, a judge wears black robes, an athlete wears sneakers, a

king wears a crown, a Christian wears a cross, and a farmer wears overalls.

36. Christ's righteousness now covers our sinful nature. God the Father now sees that righteousness, which not only covers us but has also been credited to us.

37. Our sinful nature with its "passions and desires" will plague us until we go to heaven, but they no longer define our identity. We now belong to Jesus. This new ownership provides for us a secure identity.

38. Answers may vary. Lead people to identify how they can positively express their faith to others through word and deed.

39. Self-centeredness, immorality, and despair are just a few of the characteristics of the "old self."

40. Love, joy, peace, patience, kindness, goodness, faithfulness, gentleness, and self-control flow from those who have been clothed by Christ through Holy Baptism.

The New You (Connect)

41. A fellow Christian struggling with his or her identity can be directed to God's unconditional love. In addition point out that Christ's righteousness covers them. Direct them back to their Baptism, where they were adopted into the family of God.

42. What people wear can define them as "yuppie," "preppie," "rebel," or "suit." But those who have put on Christ in Baptism are truly children of God. They not only wear Christ; their identity comes from Christ.

43. The white cloth presented to a child at Baptism signifies that this child has now put on Christ and is clothed with Christ's righteousness. The baptized child or adult now makes a "fashion statement" for Christ.

Flaunt Your Faith (Vision)

Urge participants to complete one or more of the suggested activities.

Why Baptize Infants?

Objectives

By the power of the Holy Spirit working through God's Word, participants will (1) affirm that even infants need the saving grace of God, (2) observe the Lord's gracious invitation to all people, including infants, and (3) confess that God gives and enables all people to receive the promises bestowed in Baptism.

Opening Worship

Sing or speak together stanza 1 of "Dearest Jesus, We Are Here" (*LW* 226).

Focus

44. Though infants cannot understand such words, they are still able to receive the blessings and benefits of their parents' love and care.

Read aloud how most objections to infant Baptism are based upon human conditions. Yet, God's grace is unconditional. Also emphasize that the direction of giving in Holy Baptism is from God to us, not from us to God.

45. We did not decide to be born. It was our parents' decision.
46. An adopted child receives the name of the parents and all the rights and privileges of the family.
47. An infant makes no decisions in the adoption process. Instead, an infant receives all the blessings and privileges from being adopted into the family simply because the family chose to adopt the infant.

Dead in Sin (Inform)

48. Sin begins at conception.

49. We inherit our sin from our parents. Ultimately, sin is inherited from Adam.

50. Christ's active obedience (keeping God's Law perfectly) and His passive obedience (paying the penalty for our disobedience on the cross) have been credited to us through faith. His obedience becomes our righteousness by God's grace through faith.

51. Jesus invites and welcomes children. They are included in the kingdom of heaven.

52. The kingdom of heaven is received by grace alone through faith alone in Christ Jesus; it is a gift to us from God, given at our Baptism.

53. Little children have the capacity for faith created by the Holy Spirit!

54. God decides and effects spiritual birth.

55. Parents can bring their children to Baptism, through which God bestows forgiveness of sins and eternal life.

Our Inheritance (Connect)

56. Children inherit sin from their parents.

57. The argument from silence actually supports the practice of infant Baptism. Since no specific prohibitions against baptizing infants exist, one is left to ask, "Why not baptize infants?" They certainly need the same forgiveness of sins as adults. And they certainly are included in our Lord's Great Commission to make disciples of all people by baptizing and teaching. Since human reason and will are by nature enemies of God, they could never be conditions for receiving God's grace.

58. The Holy Spirit can and does create faith wherever and in whomever He pleases (John 3:5–8). Luther wrote in his explanation to the Third Article of the Apostles' Creed, "I believe that I cannot by my own reason or strength believe in Jesus Christ, my Lord, or come to Him; but the Holy Spirit has called me by the Gospel, enlightened me with His gifts, sanctified and kept me in the true faith." The Holy Spirit

is present and at work in Baptism. Therefore, He can and does create faith in infants through this means of grace.

The Family and Faith (Vision)

Urge participants to complete one or more of the suggested activities.

Living the New Life

Objectives

By the power of the Holy Spirit working through God's Word, participants will (1) affirm that the Holy Spirit is responsible for both new life (created in Baptism) and new living; (2) describe how this new life in Christ translates into a change of heart, mind, and behavior; and (3) confess the importance of remembering one's Baptism so as to live a new life with joy.

Opening Worship

Sing or speak together stanza 1 of "Let Us Ever Walk with Jesus" (*LW* 381).

Focus

Read aloud the introduction. Note how an identity crisis often results in sporadic and even pathological behavior. Security in one's identity, on the other hand, provides for more consistent and appropriate behavior. Baptism provides us with a very secure identity.

59. Remembering our roots draws our attention to our core (often familial) identity. "Remember your roots" is often suggested when we have strayed from our original life course.

60. Answers will vary. Loving, kind, clear conscience, peaceful, and forgiving may be some of the attitudes listed. Serving, encouraging, and following God's Law may be some of the actions.

New Creation (Inform)

61. God made His light shine in our hearts. He creates our new life in Christ.

62. The lighted candle often presented at Baptism symbolizes that God's light now shines in the heart of the one baptized. It also reminds us to live in that light daily.

A Change for the Better (Connect)

63. In Baptism God comes to us in love. This love then changes our hearts, enabling and motivating us to love God.

64. Christ's righteousness is credited to us in Holy Baptism. We now can turn our attention to that righteousness and all else that is above in Christ.

65. In Baptism we become connected to the vine, that is Jesus Christ. As branches, we now live out that connection in acts of love and service.

66. We can remember that at our Baptism we received the promise of forgiveness of sins, eternal life, and the gift of the Holy Spirit.

67. By meeting on a regular basis with fellow Christians in prayer, Bible study, and worship, we are enabled by God to remember with joy the promises we received in our Baptism.

One in Christ

68. The Holy Spirit created our new life in Christ and also sustains it. The Holy Spirit has promised to come to us regularly through God's Word and Sacrament. Therefore, regular contact with such Word and Sacrament provides us with the Holy Spirit's continued guidance.

69. Possible answers may include improved relationships with spouse and children, a better attitude at work or school, and a more intentional and sincere worship life.

70. The Invocation reminds us of God's presence in our lives. The Confession and Absolution remind us of the promise of forgiveness we received in Baptism. The reading of God's Word

reminds us that the Word gives Baptism its power and promise. The Lord's Supper strengthens our faith given in the Sacrament of Baptism. The Benediction reminds us to live in the peace and joy of our baptismal promise.

Created for Life (Vision)

Urge participants to complete one or more of the suggested activities.

Appendix of Lutheran Teaching

Below you will find examples of how the first Lutherans addressed the issue of Baptism. They will help you understand the Lutheran difference.

The Augsburg Confession of 1530

Philip Melanchthon, a lay associate of Dr. Martin Luther, wrote the Augsburg Confession to clarify for Emperor Charles V just what Lutherans believed. Melanchthon summarized Lutheran teaching from the Bible and addressed the controversies of the day. This confession remains a standard of Lutheran teaching.

Article IX.1–2: Of Baptism

Of Baptism they [our churches] teach that it is necessary to salvation, and that through Baptism is offered the grace of God; and that children are to be baptized, who, being offered to God through Baptism, are received into God's grace (*Concordia Triglotta*, p. 47).

The Smalcald Articles of 1537

To prepare for a general church council, some German princes asked Dr. Martin Luther to draw up a statement of faith. These articles, which dealt with Christian teaching and specific controversies, gained popularity and became a standard of Lutheran teaching.

Part III.V: Of Baptism

Baptism is nothing else than the Word of God in the water, commanded by His institution, or, as Paul says, *a washing in the Word;* as also Augustine says: *Let the Word come to the element, and it becomes a Sacrament.* And for this reason we do not hold with Thomas and the monastic preachers [or Dominicans] who forget the Word (God's institution) and say that God has imparted to the water a spiritual power, which through the water washes away sin. Nor [do we agree] with Scotus and the Barefooted monks [Minorites or Franciscan monks], who teach that, by the assistance of the divine will, Baptism washes away sins, and that this ablution occurs only through the will of God, and by no means through the Word or water.

Of the baptism of children we hold that children ought to be baptized. For they belong to the promised redemption made through Christ, and the Church should administer it [Baptism and the announcement of that promise] to them (*Concordia Triglotta*, pp. 491–93).

The Large Catechism

The Large Catechism of Dr. Martin Luther sprang from a series of sermons he preached to help his congregation understand the basic teachings of the Bible. It serves as a companion for pastors and teachers as they explain Luther's Small Catechism.

Part IV:47–86 Of Infant Baptism

Here a question occurs by which the devil, through his sects, confuses the world, namely, *Of Infant Baptism*, whether children also believe, and are justly baptized. Concerning this we say briefly: Let the simple dismiss this question from their minds, and refer it to the learned. But if you wish to answer, then answer thus: —

That the Baptism of infants is pleasing to Christ is sufficiently proved from His own work, namely, that God sanctifies many of them who have been thus baptized, and has given them the Holy Ghost; and that there are yet many even to-day in whom we perceive that they have the Holy Ghost both because of their doctrine and life; as it is also given to us by the grace of God that we can explain the Scriptures and come to the knowledge of Christ, which is impossible without the Holy Ghost. . . .

Further, we say that we are not so much concerned to know whether the person baptized believes or not; for on that account Baptism does not become invalid; but everything depends upon the Word and command of God. This now is perhaps somewhat acute, but it rests entirely upon what I have said, that Baptism is nothing else than water and the Word of God in and with each other, that is, when the Word is added to the water, Baptism is valid, even though faith be wanting. For my faith does not make Baptism, but receives it. . . .

Lastly, we must also know what Baptism signifies, and why God has ordained just such external sign and ceremony for the Sacrament by which we are first received into the Christian Church. But the act or ceremony is this, that we are sunk under the water, which passes over us, and afterwards are drawn out again. These two parts, to be sunk under the water and drawn out again, signify the power and operation of Baptism which is nothing else than putting to death the old Adam, and after that the resurrection of the new man, both of which must take place in us all our lives, so that a truly Christian life is nothing else than a daily baptism, once begun and ever to be continued. For this must be practised without ceasing, that we ever keep purging away whatever is of the old Adam, and that that which belongs to the new man come forth (*Concordia Triglotta,* pp. 743–49).

Glossary

Baptism. From the Greek word meaning "to immerse" or "to wash." Many religions have religious washings. But Christian Baptism applies water "in the name of the Father and of the Son and of the Holy Spirit" as described by Jesus (Matthew 28:19). In Baptism God washes away the person's sins and welcomes that person as a member of His kingdom.

covenant. A relationship or agreement not based on kinship. A contract.

Essenes. A Jewish sect from the time of Christ that emphasized simplicity, purity, sacred meals, and fixed times of prayer. The community that produced the Dead Sea Scrolls was probably Essene.

Filioque. Literally, "and the Son" in Latin. This phrase was added to the Nicene Creed in the West to emphasize that the Holy Spirit proceeds from the Father *and the Son.*

godparent. A traditional term for baptismal sponsors, a person who makes required professions and promises in the name of infants or converts presented for Christian Baptism. A baptismal sponsor should encourage and support the newly baptized person in the Christian faith.

justification. God declares sinners to be just or righteous for Christ's sake; that is, God has imputed or charged our sins to Christ and He imputes or credits Christ's righteousness to us.

kingdom of God. God's rule or reign. The church is God's kingdom on earth.

means of grace. The means by which God gives us the forgiveness, life, and salvation won by the death and resurrection of Christ: the Gospel, Baptism, and the Lord's Supper.

mode of Baptism. The manner in which water is applied in Baptism: immersion, pouring (affusion), or sprinkling.

ordinance. Literally, something ordered or commanded.

polemical. From the Greek word for "battle." The term describes conversation or writing that attacks and refutes.

repentance. Sorrow for sin caused by the condemnation of the Law. Sometimes *repentance* is used in a broad way to describe all of conversion, including faith in God's mercy.

Sacrament. Literally, something sacred. In the Lutheran church, a Sacrament is a sacred act that (1) was instituted by God, (2) has a visible element, and (3) offers the forgiveness of sins earned by Christ. The Sacraments include Baptism, the Lord's Supper, and also Absolution (if one counts the pastor as the visible element).

sanctification. The spiritual growth that follows justification by grace through faith in Christ.

sponsor. See *godparent.*